Endorsement

"Great stuff here! Beating a needed drum that calls us to community and a shared life. Pity people are so entrenched in religion and its many trappings like pastors, buildings, and power.

> What I would like you to think about is that it is very, very important to feel safe. And one of the things that I am more and more aware of is how important it is for you, for me, for us to have a safe place. Where can you be really safe? Somehow the spiritual journey is a journey that requires that we have a deep, deep sense of safety. (Henri Nouwen)

I love the Safe Place idea and I have shared this for years, but the safe place becomes dangerous when people decide to go their own way once again. I would say the ekklesia is often more of a rehab setting than a healthy family. A family with problems is more usual. Damaged people together in Jesus. Then we could find a few who are mature enough to love and to forgive … those who have jettisoned their exit strategy … those in for the long haul.

I think what we need is first the resurrection and then let's do community. I think it might be easier.

You are the best. I wish we had met earlier. You complete me!"

— **Doug Heffernan**
Cork, Ireland

First Edition

Cover artwork by Kristen Hollinger
Cover design and layout by Rafael Polendo (polendo.net)

Biblical citations are taken from *The New American Standard Bible*, modified by Jon Zens, and *The New Living Translation*, modified by Jon Zens.

ISBN 978-1-938480-97-3

This volume is printed on acid free paper and meets ANSI Z39.48 standards.

Printed in the United States of America

 QUOIR

Published by Quoir
Oak Glen, California
www.quoir.com

We Are Christ on Earth

The Visible Expression of Jesus in Space and Time

Jon Zens

Dedication

I dedicate this book to Dotty, my exquisite wife of fifty-three years. The brightness of Christ flows out of her wherever she goes. His life in her has encouraged me in all our years together. When Dotty meets and bonds with the people she meets, they know that Christ is on earth in people like her.

Acknowledgements

Heartfelt gratitude and thanks go to my dear friends Mark Evans, Alison Hardy, Mary Ellen Robinson, Catherine Seebald and Charlene Wilder, for their hard work in making this a better manuscript. Over and over, I have seen the value of having many eyes look at the same pages!

Table of Contents

Foreword

I love Jon Zens...I love the way he cares for the Body of Christ. What is interesting to me is that the Lord would choose a man with such depth in theology and history of the Church to be a pioneer for practical, daily, fleshed out simplicity in Christ. Sounds like the Lord to me. Only the Lord can get the Glory in that!

In a world where doctrines and methods are debated at every turn, you have picked up a book that cuts through untested rhetoric and theories like a hot knife to butter. Two things pop out to the casual reader; this writer has years of experience and he loves to share with others the teachings, books and comments that have affected his life. When Jon says All of Christ from All His Body he is not kidding. The book is greatly strengthened by the testimonies of those in the Body of Christ who have spoken about His Ekklesia, the visible expression of the Lord Jesus Christ in this world.

Reminds me of the Bible verse in Matthew 13:52:

> He said to them, "Therefore every scribe who has become a disciple of the kingdom of heaven is like the head of a household, who brings out of his treasure things that are new and fresh and things that are old and familiar."

I have been walking out an expression of Organic Life now for over 15 years. I can testify that in my journey I have read and written many articles and books about the Organic /Simple *Ekklesia* journey. I can tell you that this will become a practical and helpful study guide for all of us looking to walk out that which we preach so much. I started to highlight the parts that spoke to me, or the things that were fresh revelation and witnessed in my spirit, and I highlighted two and three times on every page.

Did I tell you I love Jon Zens? Well, I tell you I love the visible expression of Christ that he both writes about in this book and that he models daily before a hurting and confused Church. May this book help you see Him, "our Lord Jesus Christ" more clearly!

Much love,

– Jose L. Bosque
author of *Fueled by Love: Filling the Empty Heart*
Webmaster, https://godsleader.com/

Chapter 1

The Crucial Piece of the Puzzle

Untold thousands of people "go to church" on Sunday and involve themselves in a multitude of religious activities. Multitudes of para-church organizations pursue the various causes dear to them. But in all the hurry-scurry of doing things in the name of God, very few ever reflect on the connection between the time their religious activities are consuming, and the revealed *heart of the Lord*. Sadly, it is like Jesus becomes a background assumption that undergirds human agendas.

Can we know our Father's heart? Without a doubt—His heart is revealed in Scripture. Shouldn't our lives be marked by a passionate pursuit of His heart, if we know it? Absolutely, but the evidence shows that very few have had a revelation of the Father's eternal purpose in the Son. Of course, it is true to say that His heart is with the poor and needy, the orphan and the widow. But the New Testament pinpoints His heart and purpose, and I would like to unpack His reality by using the revelation of Christ in the book of Ephesians.

The Lord did not create earth and humans willy-nilly, or out of the blue. Father, Son and Spirit had determined a plan before creation. Jesus, we are told, was a Lamb slain before the foundation of the world. Our names were written in the Lamb's book of life before anything was created.

Paul said in Ephesians 1, "For He chose us in Him before the creation of the world to be holy and blameless in His sight … And He made known to us the mystery of His will according to His good pleasure, which He purposed in Christ … In Him we were also chosen, having been predestined according to the plan of Him who works out everything in conformity with the purpose of His will … "

There is, then, a purpose in Jesus being worked out in history, "according to His eternal purpose which He accomplished in Christ Jesus" (Eph. 3:11). If we do not understand that there is a Christ-centered purpose behind all that happens, our lives will be stunted in all directions. Most religious activities are pursued with very little, if any, consciousness of His "eternal purpose in Christ." The eternal purpose must be the foundation as we work out the life God has given us. Why? Because this purpose in His Son is His *heart*.

And what is the goal of this Son-centered purpose? To bring a Bride to Jesus that is made up of people from all over the globe. Paul said that the Father wished to create an *ekklesia* on earth that would carry out His intentions in space and time. Paul saw his service to Christ in light of this purpose.

> "Although I am less than the least of all God's people, this grace was given me to preach to the Gentiles the unsearchable riches of Christ, and to make plain to everyone the outworking of this mystery, which for ages past was kept hidden in God who created all things. His intent was that now through the *ekklesia*, the many-dimensioned wisdom of God should be made known to the rulers and authorities in the heavenly realms, according to His eternal purpose which He accomplished in Christ Jesus our Lord" (Eph. 3:8-10).

The *ekklesia* is the earthly setting where Christ's life can be expressed and displayed. The *ekklesia* is to be an upside-down community, where the poly-sided wisdom of God can be showcased in innumerable ways, but especially by a loving community consisting of all races, with no regard for male/female, economic level, educational attainment or social status. It is the Lord's heart for such Christ-centered, face-to-face *ekklesias* to spring up all over the earth. Is the working out of our lives in line with His revealed heart?

To say there is a whole lot going on in the world every moment is a vast understatement. As the Lord is guiding things according to His eternal counsel, what or who is at the center of His thoughts? The answer is found in Ephesians 1:22-23.

And God placed all things under His feet and appointed Him to be Head over everything *for the sake of the ekklesia*, which is His body, the fullness of Him who fills everything in every way.

This is a beyond mind-boggling perspective! Everything from a bird falling to the ground to the rising and falling of kingdoms is happening with reference to Christ's care for the *ekklesia*. As we see wars, famines, natural disasters, political unrest, and everything else going on, we must remember that behind all of this is Christ's guiding of all things with reference to His Bride on earth. Again, all of this underscores where the heart of the Godhead rests and centers. Is this our heart too?

The seal of the Father is on the Son. The voice out of the cloud on the Mount of Transfiguration said, "This is My Beloved Son, hear Him." Everything about His heart in the eternal purpose is concerning the Son. And Jesus rules everything with reference to caring for His Bride as she carries out His life on earth.

In pages 233-305 of his book *From Eternity to Here*, Frank Viola has carved out some of the most beautiful and profound language to capture how our daily lives should be shaped by the Lord's eternal purpose in His Son:

> In so many modern churches, a set of doctrines, a certain theology, a charismatic personality, a set of special works or ministries, is the centrality rather than Christ. Mark it down: The centrality of anything other than Christ is a betrayal of the new species.

> All of the churches and movements I was involved in had effectively preached to me an "it." Evangelism is an "it." The power of God is an "it." Eschatology is an "it." Christian theology is an "it." Christian doctrine is an "it." Faith is an "it." Apologetics is an "it." Healing and deliverance are "its."

> I made the striking discovery that I don't need an "it." I have never needed an "it." And I will never need an "it." Christian "its," no matter how good or true, eventually wear out, run dry, and become tiresome.

> I don't need an "it," I need a Him! And so do you. We do not need "things." We need Jesus Christ.

> You can chase spiritual things until you are blue in the face. And there will always be some Christian who is peddling a new "it" or "thing" upon which to center your life. Warning: If you buy into it, you will most certainly miss Him.

> God's object from first to last is His Son. It is Christ—and Christ alone—that God the Father desires for His people. When the Father gives us something, it's always His Son. When the Son gives us something, it's always Himself.

> This insight greatly simplifies the Christian life. Instead of seeking many spiritual things, we seek only Him. Our single occupation is the Lord Jesus Christ. He becomes our only pursuit. We do not seek divine things; we seek a divine person. We do not seek gifts; we seek the giver who embodies all the gifts. We do not seek truth; we seek the incarnation of all truth.

As the community of the King, the church stands in the earth as the masterpiece of that reconciliation and the pilot project of the reconciled universe. In the church, therefore, the Jewish-Gentile barrier has been demolished, as well as all barriers of race, culture, sex, etc. (Gal. 3:28; Eph. 2:16). The church lives and acts as the new humanity on earth that reflects the community of the Godhead. As Stanley Grenz once put it, "The church is the pioneer community. It points toward the future God has in store for His creation" (*From Eternity to Here*, David C. Cook, 2009).

If you listen carefully to Bible teachings on radio, TV, and in pulpits, I think you will discover that the connective tissue of the "eternal purpose in Christ" is missing. Do teachers/preachers' approach at all the topics they deal with—marriage, the Christian life, abortion, church programs, last days, Israel, etc.—through the lens of the Lord's eternal purpose? How can we talk about anything without asking, how does this relate to His *heart*—His Son-centered eternal purpose?

Chapter 2

We Are Christ on Earth

One of the most striking, amazing, humbling and far-reaching revelations in the New Testament is *the relational solidarity* of Jesus and His people. When we are called "the body of Christ," this is not just a picture—it is a *reality*. We are His body on this planet. Consider these mind-boggling perspectives.

"And he fell to the earth, and heard a voice say to him, 'Saul, Saul, why are you persecuting Me?' And he said, 'Who are you, Lord?' And the Lord said, 'I am Jesus who you are persecuting'" (Acts 8:4-5). When Paul arrested and hurt believers, he was touching Christ Himself.

"Now I rejoice in what was suffered for you and I fill up in my flesh what is still lacking in regard to Christ's afflictions, for the sake of His body, which is the *ekklesia*. I have become its servant by the commission God gave me to present to you the word of God in its fullness—the mystery—that has been kept hidden for ages and generations, but is now disclosed to the saints. To them God has chosen to make known among the Gentiles the glorious riches of this mystery, which is Christ in you, the hope of glory" (Col. 1:24-27).

There is a vital sense in which Jesus' afflictions were "finished" on the cross. However, there is also the reality that in the

Lord's eternal purpose, His afflictions continue to be fulfilled in His body. Just as He suffered first in crucifixion and then entered into glory via resurrection, so His *ekklesia* continues His sufferings in this age, and then enters glory through resurrection in the age to come.

"The body is a unit, though it is made up of many parts; and though all its parts are many, they form one body. So it is with Christ" (1 Cor. 12:12). Paul says something that is jarring— Jesus is interchangeable with His body.

Let's reflect a bit on what occurred at the end of Jesus' earthly life. As He knew His leaving the disciples and returning to His Father was imminent, He announced to them, "But you know the Spirit, for He lives with you and will be in you. I will not leave you as orphans; I will come to you ... On that day you will realize that I am in My Father, and you are in Me, and I am in you ... You heard Me say, 'I am going away and I am coming back to you.'"

Many have attributed Jesus' words, "I will come to you," to indicate His final coming at the end of the age. But by taking this position, something very important is skipped over and missed. *Jesus was referring to His coming in the Spirit to the ekklesia on the Day of Pentecost*—"He has received from the Father the promised Holy Spirit and has poured out what you now see and hear" (Acts 2:33).

On the Day of Pentecost Jesus came to His waiting remnant in the Spirit's power, and then His *ekklesia* would continue His ministry on earth until His final return to usher in a New Heaven and New Earth. Truly, Jesus' Bride is now *Christ on earth*, being His hands, feet, eyes, ears and His heart to one another, and to a fallen, hurting world. Frank Viola hones in on our place in God's eternal purpose:

Now let me ask: What is the purpose of a body? The answer: to express the life that's within it. My body gives my personality expression. In the same way, the physical body of Jesus was the instrument, or the tool, for God to manifest His personality in the earth.

What had taken place [on the Day of Pentecost]? The body of Christ was born on the earth. But what does that mean? It means this: The literal body of Jesus Christ had returned to earth. It expanded; God now had a family.

Jesus Christ in heaven had dispensed Himself into His body on earth. He returned to earth in the form of His body, the church, and His species was reintroduced to the planet.

In the eyes of God, the Church is nothing more and nothing less than Jesus Christ on earth. It's a new species that's kin to divinity; a body to the Son and a family to the Father. Kind of His own kind *(From Eternity to Here)*.

An event in a dingy Romanian prison years ago highlights this point. Richard Wurmbrand was standing in a cell with fifty men. After being together for a number of days, one of the men looked Richard in the eyes and said, "Are you Jesus Christ?" His first inclination was to say, "No." But with a moment's thought he replied, "Yes."

Chapter 3

The Forgotten Horizontal Dimension of His Cross in Ephesians 2

Traditional systematic theologies have dealt with Christ's cross-work primarily in terms of its *vertical* dimension—that He died to heal the alienation between the Creator and humanity. This aspect of Golgotha is indeed vital and foundational.

But the New Testament goes further to reveal the multi-dimensional realities of the Cross. The *cosmic* dimension is found in Col. 2, the *charismatic* dimension is found in Eph. 4, and the *communal* (horizontal) dimension is revealed in places like Eph. 2 and 1 Cor. 12:13.

Francis Schaeffer called this horizontal dimension the "sociological healing" that flows out of Gospel salvation. In other words, as each individual is baptized by the Spirit into Christ, they also come into His body, where there is no Jew or Greek, bond or free, or male and female (1 Cor. 12:13).

This *ekklesia* setting, then, becomes the "display case" of God's multi-faceted grace and wisdom (Eph. 3:10). Thus, in the

New Testament, salvation is not *individualistic* (people saved *alone*), but rather *corporate* (people in relationship *with others*).

In Ephesians 2, Paul pointed out that the Law required that Jew and Gentile be kept apart. Jesus came, honored and fulfilled the Law, then took away the barrier of the Law so that the two would be one in a "new humanity."

> For He Himself is our peace, who made both *groups into* one and broke down the barrier of the dividing wall, by abolishing in His flesh the hostility, *which is* the Law *composed* of commandments *expressed* in ordinances, so that in Himself He might make the two one new person, *in this way* establishing peace; and that He might reconcile them both in one body to God through the cross, by it having put to death the hostility. And He came and preached peace to you who were far away, and peace to those who were near; for through Him we both have our access in one Spirit to the Father (*NASB*).

From this context, we can see that it is crucial to affirm both that Jesus died to atone for our sins (vertically, toward God), and that He died to create a "new person" (horizontally in relationships), which was the culmination of His eternal purpose in Christ.

Tragically, and for a number of reasons, the centrality of this horizontal fabric of the believer's life has been virtually forgotten. Consider, for example, the content of most gospel tracts. The focus is on "getting saved," but nothing is said about the fact that in this new life *they are to function in His body by the Spirit.*

Why has this horizontal dimension slipped away from Evangelical consciousness? Church history pretty much answers this question.

In the period of 150AD to 300AD, body ministry was gradually replaced by an increasing fixation and dependence on *church leaders.*

With the advent of Constantine around 325AD, the visible church became intertwined with civil politics. The church became more and more institutionalized, and saw herself as the dispenser of salvation through the sacraments. Lost was the whole perspective of the *ekklesia* being a counter-cultural community.

During the Middle Ages, people from cradle to grave were under the thumb of the church, doing whatever they were told by the hierarchy out of fear.

The Protestant Reformation brought some light as to how people gain right standing with God, but they did not break with State backing, and their conception of the priesthood of all believers was *individualistic*, and was overshadowed by the emphasis on "ministers."

With the advent of the printing press, the absolute power the church had over people was broken; since around AD 1600 religious groups then proliferated.

The Anabaptists were one of these groups. Through their study of the New Testament, they came to embrace and practice the *communal/horizontal* nature of the *ekklesia*.

The 17th Century Puritan movement in England became obsessed with church members wrestling with their personal interest in Christ, and each person "making their calling and election sure."

This was the primary theology that made its way to American shores around 1620-30. Then as the New Land began to expand Westward, a rugged individualism emerged. The evangelistic methods that surfaced in the 19th Century in Charles Finney and Dwight Moody moved away from the harshness of Puritanism, and the emphasis fell on a more direct relationship with God by people coming forward in response to altar calls.

While there were, of course, exceptions, the religion of America was for the most part oblivious to the *communal life of the ekklesia*. It was about *one's personal relationship*, not the *corporate expression of Christ among living stones*.

It is therefore of great significance and encouragement to note that since the mid-1960's a growing number of voices have articulated the obvious New Testament concern that the *ekklesia* be a *thriving organism*, not an *institution* to be preserved.

A book that years ago opened up my awareness of the horizontal dimension of the cross was John Driver's *Understanding the Atonement for the Mission of the Church* (Herald Press, 1986). This work deserves your attention if you wish to explore further this dimension of Jesus' work.

What are some implications of the horizontal/communal dimension of the Cross for our practice of *ekklesia*? It seems to me that one of the key implications would be that *in our living and in our presentation of the Gospel we consciously connect new life in Christ with life in His ekklesia*.

In other words, we are not just asking people to say a prayer and invite Jesus into their heart. Instead, we are inviting them to a full-orbed life of following Christ—a life of knowing Christ and functioning with the brothers and sisters in His body. This organic reality entails a whole lot more than just "going to church."

Another implication would be that Jesus-communities should be displaying the Lord's goal of "the two being made one"—fellowships where Jew and Gentile, male and female, slave and free, rich and poor, educated and uneducated can all follow Jesus together in fervent love.

That is why Paul had to correct Peter publicly: his removing of himself from table fellowship with believing Gentiles when certain friends of James came, contradicted the "sociological healing" that a watching world should see in the New Humanity.

Realizing that horizontal realities are embedded in Christ's cross opens up new vistas for understanding issues the early church faced. For example, in post-apostolic times the Lord's supper became an individualistic ritual where believers examined themselves regarding sin in their life. But when Paul told each of the Corinthians to "examine themselves," the context indicates that he had in view *one's relationship to others in the body*. The way they were coming together reflected schism, not bondedness. They were not eating together as a unit. The poor were thereby being humiliated. The giving nature of Christ was not reflected in the way they shared food with one another. In such circumstances, the Supper could only be done *"unworthily"* because the way they were acting was a denial of all that it signified. If we miss the social dimensions of the cross—the New Humanity—the New Testament will always be a veiled book to us in crucial ways.

The movement in post-apostolic times from vibrant body-life to dependence on leaders, from Spirit-led ministry to institutionalized forms, and from free-flowing relationships to political backing and intrigue all combined to eliminate any consciousness of the horizontal/relational purposes the Lord had in Jesus' cross-work. The horizontal healing accomplished by Jesus' cross was largely buried and forgotten.

We should, therefore, be encouraged by the emergence of sensitivity to, and concern for, the body dimension of the believer's life in Christ, as evidenced by the books, talks and articles on the subject. May the Lord give us grace to make intentional efforts to see this vital aspect of Christ's work become rooted in the life of His *ekklesias*.

The essence of this chapter was presented at the *Elemental Conference*, held in Toronto, Canada, in April, 2017.

Chapter 4

The Cross in the Community

The importance of the cross in the life of a local *ekklesia*, as well as in each of the individuals involved, cannot be overstated. Frank Viola addresses this issue beautifully in the following pages, which are taken from a transcript of a message he delivered at the 2009 *Reimagining Church Conference* in Toronto, Canada.

– JZ

Having an Instinct for the Cross

By Frank Viola

Living with other Christians in community is one of the most glorious experiences a Christian can know. But it doesn't work, it never has worked, and it never will work unless you embrace the cross.

Living with the saints in heaven will be glory; living with the saints on earth is another story.

I've spoken on the cross of Jesus Christ countless times. But when I speak on "bearing the cross," I'm not talking about the Lord's atoning death for us.

I'm rather speaking about the principle of the cross … the principle of dying to oneself.

The cross has to do with denying our fallen soul life, or what some theologians call "the self life." This is your basic nature of self-interest, self-perseverance, and self-defense.

In Luke 9:23-24, Jesus is speaking about the denial of our fallen nature saying,

> And he said to them all, If any man will come after me, let him deny himself, and take up his cross daily, and follow me. For whosoever will save his life shall lose it: but whosoever will lose his life for my sake, the same shall save it.

Paul also referred to the cross in 1 Corinthians 15:31 and 2 Corinthians 4:8-12.

These texts are not speaking of salvation. They are speaking about picking up a cross, carrying that cross daily, and following Christ in the denial of oneself.

Brothers and sisters, there's a cross for all of us.

And God calls each of us to bear the cross of Christ.

Thus whenever your ego is touched, whenever your pride is exposed, whenever your weaknesses are pointed out, the cross is ready to do its deep work.

And you can either fight against it or die upon it.

A PERSONAL REFERENCE

Forgive the personal reference, but when I was 20 years old, many of my peers—and those older than me—would tell me that God had gifted me in unusual ways. I didn't realize at the time that this meant that God would have to break me in some major ways so that I would be truly useful for His service.

So I was an unbroken vessel … just like most Christians in their early 20s. (Unfortunately, many gifted people remain unbroken throughout most of their lives because they repeatedly resist the cross when it comes into their lives.)

However, God in His mercy brought the cross into my life in ways that I could have never anticipated ... and the result was utter devastation to my self-life. I became a different person on all fronts.

Consequently, the lessons I'm sharing with you in this message have come out of the anvil of much suffering, much breaking, and much pain. They have come out of an experience of the cross in my own life.

In that connection, I feel that one should never speak on this dimension of the cross unless they themselves have had a steady diet of all its darkness and horrendous depths. If not, what they share will only be bloodless theory and have little impact on people's lives.

10 INSIGHTS ABOUT THE CROSS

1. A person cannot teach you how to recognize the cross in your life. God must show you. It's a matter of spiritual instinct.

2. The ears of God's people tend to be deaf to the cross. We don't like to hear about it.

3. The cross is the easiest thing in the world to forget. So we need to be reminded of it.

4. You will never know the Lord you're supposed to know outside of a head-on collision with His cross.

5. Authentic body life never works the way you want it to. It's a railroad track to the cross.

6. The instrument of the cross is very often our fellow brethren in Christ.

7. You cannot crucify yourself. You can drive one nail into one hand, but the other hand will be free. So the cross is God's wonderful design.

8. God will create a tailor-made cross for you. Jesus is a carpenter, so He knows how to build them. And very often, the cross will be served to you freely by your brothers and sisters with whom you fellowship.

9. The more gifted you are, the more the cross is needed in your life to break your tendency to rely on yourself, to manipulate, and to exalt yourself in subtle ways.

10. In community, your blind spots will eventually get exposed. True body life is a house of mirrors. The Lord will not destroy the Lord within you, but He'll seek to destroy everything else. This is especially true if He has called you to His work.

LESSONS ON THE CROSS FROM THE OLD TESTAMENT

The Altar. In the tabernacle of Moses, the altar is the first piece of furniture you came to before you got to God's house. The altar is the place of death. It's the place of sacrifice and the loss of a life. The altar always precedes the house.

Therefore, in order for God's house to be built, it requires someone who has known the cross in their experience and died upon it. Everyone who builds God's house in the New Testament was a person who was shattered and devastated by the cross.

For God's house to be maintained, the living stones who make it up must also accept a steady diet of the cross. They must learn to deny themselves, to give themselves to the exposing work of the Spirit to break and sift them, and to refuse to fight against it.

Church splits take place because some aren't willing to bear the cross. They will start maligning certain people when their feelings are hurt or they are offended. Thus the carnage produced by unbroken, self-centered vessels is great.

The Temple of Solomon. Solomon's temple was made up of stones. But there was no mortar to glue them together. Rather, the stones were held together by friction.

That meant that each stone had to be cut, chiseled, sanded, and shaped to fit the others perfectly.

The words of Paul and Peter about being "built together" come to mind. Being built together with other believers requires the chiseling and cutting work of the cross.

Remember, Calvary preceded Pentecost.

Calvary is the place of the cross; Pentecost is where the church is born.

The cross precedes the church. And it's maintained by the cross.

Romans 6 is all about the cross. And it precedes Romans 12, which is all about the church.

So in the center of the *ekklesia* … in the dead middle of Christian community … there is a cross that bids each of us to die.

In community, after the honeymoon period ends, you will find the cross in spades.

I've described body life many times as a wedding of glory and gore. The glory precedes the gore at first, then the gore precedes the greater glory.

The cross has many corners. And it never comes in the package you want.

THE PROBLEM OF HURT FEELINGS

Let me tell you the way that many Christians live their lives.

When (not if) they get their feelings hurt, they make decisions ... sometimes rash and self-serving decisions ... based on their bruised feelings.

They form their opinions, their reactions, and their attitudes around their feelings when those feelings have been injured.

And so they run from the cross.

What does this do? It delays their transformation on the one hand, and brings devastation to other people's lives on the other.

Hence, the most toxic people on the planet are those who will lash out against those who they believe have hurt their feelings.

We have ways of wiggling out of the cross that would drive a battery of mental professionals nutty.

But the Lord gains the most ground in us when we're looking down from a cross.

Mark it down: If there is ever a time in your life to deny yourself and lose, it's when you feel someone has hurt your feelings.

It's when someone corrects you in Christ, but you don't wish to receive the correction or don't understand it.

It's when someone strongly disagrees with you.

It's when you correct someone in Christ, and they not only reject it, but they retaliate by trying to defame you.

It's when someone hates you out of jealousy, and with malice in their hearts, spreads vicious lies about you.

It's when someone doesn't meet your expectations.

Each case is when the cross seeks to do its deepest work in your life.

Christians who take offense resist the cross.

Christians who retaliate to protect their own reputations and self interests, not caring about the damage they bring into the lives of others, know nothing of the cross.

The reaction of the flesh is always to defend, to justify, to get angry, to lash out, to retaliate.

Sometimes it's done in passive aggressive ways. And it's virtually always justified by "religious talk" under the cloak of "God told me."

The flesh will never sacrifice itself or absorb the blows. It will instead be quick to sacrifice others on the altar of one's feelings.

The flesh always seeks to protect one's ego and reputation in the eyes of others and at the expense of others.

Those who do not know the cross cannot tolerate loss, suffering, or correction. They cannot remain silent, as the Lord Jesus was silent under pressure.

They cannot wait on the Lord nor submit to His light. They will rather allow themselves to react in the flesh, and they will even call their reaction "being led by the Spirit."

But this is deception.

These reactions are the fruit of an unbroken person who has made themselves the priority, refusing to take the high road which is what the spirit of the Lamb will always lead us to do.

Brethren, you can waste the Lord's transformation in your life by fighting the cross.

The cross of Christ bids us to die, to lose, to surrender. The flesh will do everything it can to stay alive and protect itself.

To this you were called, because Christ suffered for you, leaving you an example, that you should follow in his steps . . . When they hurled their insults at him, he did not retaliate; when he suffered, he made no threats. Instead, he entrusted himself to him who judges justly.

According to Peter, following in Jesus' footsteps means that when we are wrongly accused or rightly corrected, we will not insult, retaliate, or make threats.

Instead, we will entrust the matter into the Lord's hands.

To make this personal . . .

If you defend yourself, God will not defend you.

If you justify yourself, God will not justify you.

All those who know the Lord deeply understand these lessons.

Jesus Christ cannot gain much ground in your life unless you are willing to lose.

Whosoever will lose his life for my sake, the same shall save it.

The fruit of such loss is less of you and more of Him.

In addition, if you bail out of those relationships that you find difficult on your flesh, then the cross will follow you through someone else, somewhere else. You can't run away from it. It will find you out.

The eleven disciples ran at break-neck speed when they saw the cross emerging on that hill. They headed for the hills while the women stayed with Jesus.

Our flesh seeks to do the same whenever the cross emerges in our lives.

A TEMPTATION FOR FRIENDS

I've watched this all my life. When the Lord brings the cross into someone's life, one of the temptations is for the undiscerning is to erect a ladder and try to pull the person down from the wood.

Others will climb on the cross and seek to put padding behind the person's head and legs.

When God has brought the cross into someone's life, you must allow Him to do His deep work in their lives without interfering. I'm not talking about comforting a person who has truly been abused or victimized; I'm speaking of a person who is resisting the cross and justifying themselves at the expense of others.

When friends seek to console a person who is trying to escape the cross, especially after they have been corrected in Christ, it only prolongs that person's death-to-self and it usually ends up turning other people into "enemies."

The result is that God's enemy has been given an open door to malign people; division and carnage are the result.

WHAT TO EXPECT WHEN YOU BEAR THE CROSS

You can expect that no one will throw roses on your grave.

No one will pin a medal on your chest for how valiantly you lost and died.

In fact, few people will even notice.

The angels will, however.

And the Lord Jesus Christ said "pick up your cross daily and follow Me."

Whenever someone speaks on the cross like this, there's usually someone who reacts saying, "Well, I'm being physically and verbally abused, does bearing the cross mean that God wants me to continue to be a door mat?"

Absolutely not. That's not what I'm speaking about. In fact, for you, the cross may very well mean separating yourself from the abuser and perhaps (if it applies) getting the authorities involved.

The cross may also mean correcting someone who is hurting others or who has a blind spot that's injurious to people. This often constitutes a cross because all lovers of Jesus absolutely despise the task of correcting others. It comes at a heavy cost, because an unbroken person will retaliate when being corrected in Christ.

THE PROBING VOICE OF GOD

The voice of the Lord not only probes our actions, but it also probes our attitudes and reactions.

And the voice of the Lord often comes to us through members of His Body.

If you desire for God to use you in His work, He will deal ruthlessly with those areas of your life that you're blind to, but that other members of the body who know you can see clearly.

And His voice will be uttered by your brothers and sisters.

When it is, it finds us out.

If you are in the flesh … you will react.

If you are in the Spirit … you will not react.

Instead, you will be like a sponge, asking questions to understand what part of your life needs the blinding light of God to expose and transform.

The way a person responds when they are corrected reveals volumes about their character.

When a little pressure is applied, it exposes who we really are.

At the slightest correction from another believer, the unbroken are quick to defend themselves and their actions.

By contrast, a person who knows the cross will take all forms of correction to heart. They will exhibit a teachable spirit.

It doesn't break their jaw to admit they did wrong, and they will be very quick to repent and apologize at the slightest word of correction.

Long lasting ministry comes out of being broken bread and poured-out wine. That's written in the bloodstream of God's universe.

The good news is there is always a resurrection on the other side of every cross. However, you will not know the power of Christ's resurrection until you've first licked the wood of the cross and known the fellowship of His sufferings.

If church history has taught us anything, it is this: If God has called you to build His house, then you *must* have an instinct for the cross. If not, He will remove His hand from your life (not of salvation, but of favor and anointing). You will go forth in your own energy and your own power to the detriment of His people and His kingdom.

You will sacrifice others to try to save yourself, your work, and your reputation.

CLOSING WORDS

I want to close this message by reading some profound words that have been attributed to Watchman Nee (though I wasn't able to verify the source):

What does it mean to go to the Cross to die to the self-life?

When you can receive correction and reproof from one of less stature than yourself and can humbly submit inwardly as well as outwardly, finding no rebellion or resentment rising up within your heart, that is dying to self.

When your good is evil spoken of, when your wishes are crossed, your advice disregarded, your opinion ridiculed, and you refuse to let anger rise in your heart, or even defend yourself, but take it all in patient loving silence, that is dying to self.

When you never care to refer to yourself in conversation, or to record your own good works, or itch after commendation, when you can truly love to be unknown, that is dying to self.

When you are forgotten, or neglected, or purposely set at naught, and you don't sting and hurt with the insult or the oversight, but your heart is happy, being counted worthy to suffer for Christ, that is dying to self.

Are you dead yet?

(Frank Viola, "The Message Most Needed, But the One Few Want to Hear," https://frankviola.org/2014/02/28/thecross/)

Chapter 5

Jesus, The Incarnation of Humility

"Who being in very nature God … made Himself nothing … humbled Himself and became obedient to death—even death on a cross!" (Philippians 2)

I've been feeling a need to speak about humility for some time. This subject has popped up on Facebook many times. Humility is a tough topic to broach. You would be very skeptical if you saw a conference advertised with the pitch—"Excelling in Humility & How I Attained It!"

Christ incarnated humility by "leaving it all" and entering earth's sin-infected space and time. His humility reached its fullest expression in the darkness of Golgotha—humiliated by taking the curse connected to hanging on a tree (Gal. 3:13; Deut. 21:22-23).

This Lord Jesus now dwells in us. Believers can, as Paul noted, "be clothed in humility." To "clothe ourselves in the Lord Jesus Christ" is to be likewise dressed in humility (Rom. 13:14).

But it must be underscored that humility will only be deepened in us to the degree that we follow Christ's pattern. For humility to blossom in our beings we must be daily acquainted with His cross. Proud persons know very little of the cross-life.

Jesus intends for His life to be expressed in the Body of Christ on earth *through face-to-face relationships*. It must be stressed that social media like Facebook cannot function as *ekklesia*. No doubt social media can be helpful to those in a wilderness season, and for communicating with those already in organic relationships. But the fact of the matter is that exchanging e-words with people you have never met is not *community* as it is unfolded in the New Testament. Smiley faces and other symbols are very dim shadows of the real shared life together among believers that Paul saw come to expression in the first century.

Perhaps understanding that the e-world can function quite well without living relationships helps us appreciate why humility is so scarce, and why pride often surfaces in the endless posting on the internet.

When I was substituting in a public high school recently, I saw a poster on the wall. It should be of interest to us that in light of the bullying, etc., that has occurred on the Internet, a program has emerged in which students are asked to "Pause Before You Post" (PBP). They are encouraged to make these commitments:

- Before I make a post, I pledge to ask myself:

- Who will be able to see what I post?

- Will anyone be embarrassed or hurt by it?

- Am I proud of what I'm posting?

- How I would feel if someone posted it about me?

(http://www.jostens.com/student/students_cp_pause_
before_you_post.html; Apparently this website no longer
exists)

Those who converse with others through social media would
do well to think on those basic points. We all need to PBP!
May I offer some fruit that will appear when the humility
of Christ is present? I think all of us would do well to carefully
consider these perspectives as we communicate with others, and
react to things people say to us in the e-world.

- People filled with Christ will speak to others in a way
  that they would want others to speak to them.

- People with the living waters of Christ flowing from their innermost being will speak words
  that bring healing not hurt. "The lips of the righ-
  teous nourish many" (Proverbs 10:21).

- Saints will be increasingly conscious that when they
  speak to believers they are in a real sense speaking to
  Jesus. Christ told Paul that when he was messing with
  His followers, he was messing with Him (Acts 9:4).

- When you read something that concerns, bothers,
  upsets or troubles you, make sure you understand
  what the other person meant and intended instead
  of retorting quickly with a combative response. Ask
  them a question like, "In these comments you made,
  am I correct in understanding you to mean this?"
  Make an inquiry instead of pouncing on someone's remarks. Explore the other's heart instead of
  assuming that you understand their position.

- True humility will not pigeonhole and label people. It is very frustrating to see arbitrary labels pinned on others, when those being so categorized are scratching their heads in disbelief.

- I think one of the most common violations of humility occurs when people say things about others publicly that they would never say to their face. And there are certainly occasions where a person should go directly to another with their concerns, and keep them out of the public arena.

- The humility of Christ will lead a person to be open to learn from many sources. Consider what is reported about Apollos in Acts 18. Here was a brother who was eloquent and savvy in the Scriptures. But when Priscilla and Aquila heard him in the synagogue, they saw that his understanding was deficient. They invited him to their home and Priscilla and Aquila "explained to him the way of God more accurately." Here's a guy that knew the Old Testament backwards and forwards, but he possessed a humility that was open to learn from a wife (who was listed first) and her husband.

- Humility will lead a person to trust the Spirit to work in hearts. "For the Lord's servant must not quarrel; instead, he/she must be kind to everyone … Those who oppose he/she must gently instruct, in the hope that God will grant them repentance … " (2 Tim. 2:25).

I leave you with some quotations from Thomas Dubay. His book, *Caring: A Biblical Theology of Community* is one of the most profound works I have ever read. I would ask that you bring these words from *Caring* to Father, and ask Him to reveal some of their implications for how you communicate with and respond to others.

"The initial task the members of the group should face is the exploration of one another's minds ... Evaluation is a later step, not the first one. Initially we should concentrate on *understanding* why the member is saying this, on exploring his/her mind."

"When a person refers to a position he does not share, he should make a conscious effort to represent that opinion fairly."

"Most of us easily assume that we listen to others. Perhaps. But perhaps not. We hear all the words and sentences, but whether we heed is another matter. Receiving sound waves from another human being requires only a normal hearing apparatus and a sufficiently wakeful state. Listening to that person is incomparably more complex. All of us, therefore, need to learn to listen."

"We need to be humble, small in our own estimation. Finding the solution to a mathematical problem is possible without humility, but finding God's will is impossible without this virtue."

"We try to grow in awareness that the person sharing is important, even precious, 'God's beloved' (Romans 1:7). We pay attention to important people. To the proud person others are not important, and so he is not inclined to take them that seriously. Even more, we value the opinions of those we love. If I do not really care what my brother/sister thinks, I had better doubt that I love my brother/sister."

Adrienne von Speyr uttered some profound thoughts about Christ's lowliness. We would do well to let her words sink into our bones.

In the foot-washing, the Lord humbles himself not only to the level of the disciples, but lower, beneath them. If the Lord wants to remove all disgrace from humans, he must place himself in a position in which one need not look up to him, but can look down to him. In this lower position that he adopts, he courts us, earnestly and urgently, and not just in passing. So low does he place himself that none of the lofty or the lowly can feel themselves passed by. The Lord in his humility will always stand lower than any other human being (*The Farewell Discourses: Meditations on John 13-17* [1948], Ignatius Press, 1987, p. 18).

In light of Frank's piece on the cross, and the words above about humility, a bit more needs to be said about *why* they are so pivotal in the building of the Lord's house. The simple truth is this: the Lord wants all the glory to be His in the *ekklesia*. In order for this to be the reality, the Bride must be crucifixion-focused and immersed in the humility flowing out of Jesus. Pride ruined the Garden of Eden, and pride will always debilitate His life among the saints.

At any given moment, those in a group are at different levels of maturity, humility and attachment to the cross in their daily lives. As I said in *Elusive Community*, "But here's where it gets tricky. Community cannot only be about people whose ducks seem to be in a row. People may come into the group who are deeply wounded, and bring with them all kinds of heavy baggage. The image of a hospital could rightly be connected to a loving community." Rosine Hammett and Loughlan Sofield add to this line of thought:

> Community groups should be therapeutic, inasmuch as they assist members to grow to the fullness of their life in Christ. People need to see a group of persons, motivated by the gospel and their love of God, who live in such a way that loneliness and alienation are dispelled ("Developing Healthy Community." R. Hammett & L. Sofield, *Searching Together*, 24:3, 1996).

Chapter 6

What Was the Early Ekklesia Like?

A.M. Fairbairn noted in 1910 concerning the early church that "regarded as to its internal relating, it was a family … in the apostles' day churches were so small that everyone knew each other and kept a watchful eye on one another." But by AD 200 the family ethos was lost and the focus shifted to leadership and increasing organization.

Carolyn Osiek and David Balch have provided one of the best crisp summaries of the cultural context and life of the First Century *ekklesia*.

> While the most luxurious houses offered a certain gracious living, the vast majority of residents of an ancient Mediterranean city or town lived lives full of hardship, poor health, and crowding, with high rates of infant mortality and low life expectancy. In this environment, earliest Christianity was born and developed. All evidence points to domestic buildings [houses] as the first sites for Christian gatherings. Even during the life of Jesus, the house seems to have been a favorite site for teaching … The first groups of his followers after his death began meeting in private houses … In these earliest years, perhaps for the first century and a half, there were probably no structural adaptations for Christian worship, but rather, the adaptation of the group to the structures available … When the group became too large, another was founded in another location … This first phase of Christian worship lasted until the middle or end of the second century, by which time numbers had grown considerably and liturgy was evolving beyond the capacity of domestic architecture to support it. No longer was the Eucharist celebrated at a common meal, but at a ritual commemoration that retained only the stylized structure of a meal … By this time, houses used as gathering places for Christian assemblies began to be remodeled into buildings better adapted for assembly and worship … Thus what was once a private house became a building devoted to Christian religious use … The separation of the Eucharist from a meal and the growing numbers of believers necessitated the removal of worship from the venue of the private dwelling, and thus *from the family setting*. From then on, Christian worship was conducted according to the profile of public liturgy and *no longer took place in a family environment*. The growing authority of the bishop concentrated more and more powers in the hands, not of local leaders, but of centralized authority

figures responsible for larger and larger groups of believers" (*Families in the New Testament World*, Mohr & Siebeck, 1997, pp. 32-35; italics mine).

Ernest F. Scott offered this picture of an early *ekklesia* gathering:

> Prayer was offered, as in the Synagogue, but not in stated liturgical form. It was uttered freely, on the impulse of the Spirit, and was presented in the name of Christ, the Intercessor ... The Christian faith gave rise to hymns of a new character, often produced in the heat of the moment and almost as soon forgotten; but sometimes short lyrics of real beauty were treasured and repeated ... Chief of all these [elements] was the observance of the Supper ... This, indeed, was not so much a part of the worship as the vessel which contained all the parts. The purpose of the Christian meeting was to hold the common meal, and to make it a memorial of Jesus' Last Supper with the disciples ... The exercise of the spiritual gifts was thus the characteristic element in primitive worship. Those gifts might vary in their nature and degree according to the capacity of each individual, but they were bestowed on all and room was allowed in the service for the participation of all who were present. "When you meet together," says Paul, "each of you hath a psalm, a teaching, a tongue, an interpretation." Every member was expected to contribute something of his own to the common worship ... Worship in those first days was independent of all forms (*The Nature of the Early Church*, Charles Scribner's Sons, 1941, pp. 75, 77, 79, 87).

These observations do not come from zealous house church advocates, but from seasoned scholars who have closely studied the New Testament environment. Church historians and theologians of all stripes agree that the early brothers and sisters met in simplicity around the Lord Jesus.

We can see from post-apostolic history the disastrous effects that occurred when the family atmosphere faded away, and organization and leaders took prominence. Should these matters not be of grave concern to us, and do they not help us understand why the visible church is so out of step with the life that comes from Jesus through His people?

Chapter 7

Expressing Christ in Organic Church

What does the life that comes from Jesus through His people look like? Can it possibly be a reality in light of how far the modern church had strayed from her roots? The following 2011 article by Mark Lake, addresses these very issues in a striking way.

–JZ

By Mark Lake

I've found that when people hear about a church that gathers without a designated leader to present a prepared sermon or teaching, it is difficult for them to imagine how else the church would gather. The pastor-pew format is so ingrained in today's church culture, it is hard to picture anything else. But there are, in fact, "organic churches" who meet together with no human person designated as her leader, where all of the saints gather together and share the riches of her Bridegroom, Jesus Christ, and allow Him to be the head of the church meeting.

Frank Viola has described organic church like this:

By "organic church," I mean a non-traditional church that is born out of spiritual life instead of constructed by human institutions and held together by religious programs. Organic church life is a grass roots experience that is marked by face-to-face community, every-member functioning, open-participatory meetings (opposed to pastor-to-pew services), non-hierarchical leadership, and the centrality and supremacy of Jesus Christ as the functional Leader and Head of the gathering.

The following illustration is how I have tried to describe what happens when an organic church meets together to express Christ with every member functioning:

Paul says in Ephesians 3:8 that there are "unsearchable riches" in Christ. Imagine with me that the Louvre Museum in Paris is a picture of all of the riches that are in Christ. The Louvre has approximately 35,000 exhibits in its massive museum grounds, not to mention that the architecture alone is stunning. Many of the most famous pieces of artwork in history are housed within these walls.

Now, imagine a group of people setting out to explore and experience the riches of this museum. To give 5 minutes to each of the 35,000 pieces of art would take 243 twelve hour days! Picture this group entering the museum in awe of its beautiful architecture. They gather around a famous art display and take in its beauty and uniqueness. After some time, they share with each other what aspects of this piece of art stood out to them and how it affected them. As they go around the group taking turns sharing, they find that no one saw quite the same thing, even though they were all certainly looking at the same piece. Some were astounded by the colors. Others were captivated by the fine detail in the work. Some were focused on one particular aspect, such as the expression on a face. Some wondered about the meaning of the painting. Others pondered the artist's motivation for the piece.

As the group shared their varied insights, everyone saw much more of the artwork than any one person saw themselves. As the group moves through the museum, gazing upon the beautiful art and sharing with each other, they grow closer as they share together, and even begin to see the artwork from other people's perspective.

Additionally, the group may decide to disperse in random directions to search out some artifact that catches their interest. They may ponder this piece alone or with just a few from the larger group. Later, the group comes back together and shares with each other what they have found. Many times, a very discernible theme will appear as they share, even though there was no intention to seek a common theme. (I've been in meetings where this happens and it is truly electrifying!) As each person shares about the treasure that they found, many different aspects of this massive museum may be revealed. The group may decide to venture together through some of these areas and behold together the treasure that some have brought to the group.

It is much the same as this when a group of people gather to express the Lord Jesus Christ together. Rather than getting only one view (such as from a pastor), many people bring many various views that are woven together into a beautiful picture of

Christ that is much more rich than only one person's view. In other words, Jesus Christ is the art piece that this group beholds.

Imagine if the same group went to the Louvre Museum, but when they made it into the foyer, they elected only one person to go in and view the artwork and then come back and share with the group what he alone saw. Without entering in to the museum together, the group's ability to fully understand what the one person saw is difficult and limited. Week after week, they gather in the foyer and listen to this one person describe more of what he has seen. As the weeks and years pass, this person appears to be so much of an expert in the Louvre artwork, the group is intimidated to think about going inside themselves, lest they be expected to come back and expound on what they saw as well as the expert does.

In my view, this is similar to what happens in a church that depends on a select few clergy to minister Christ. Certainly, there are many pastors and clergy members who have a great depth of knowledge of Christ and a rich relationship with Him. But when the duty of exploring Him rests completely or mostly on the clergy's shoulders, the rest of the body becomes passive and underdeveloped. In an organic expression of the church (as I've defined here), this duty is shared among the priesthood of *all* believers.

You may read this and not believe that Christians can live in this way together with each other. I can affirm by experience that they can, but only when their focus is learning together how to live by Christ's indwelling life. But that, of course, is another story for another day.

Mark Lake, 2011

Chapter 8

Christ Expressed Together

"Church attendance is down—offerings are
down … Members of the Church Council, it's
time for another Prophecy Conference."

Years ago Dotty and I were in a gathering of saints where Christ
blossomed in a totally unexpected way. His presence was surely
not connected to any human planning or human leadership.
This group met in an old school building. That morning everything went wrong. People were standing outside on a cold, damp
morning, waiting for the janitor to show up with the key—forty
minutes late. Then, once inside, it was discovered that no one
had a key to open the storage room that contained the chairs,

songbooks, and other items necessary to set up for the meeting. Getting the room opened took another fifteen minutes. Needless to say, by then most brothers and sisters had become edgy and frustrated.

But there was also a deeply emotional dimension to this particular get-together. A cloud of sorrow and confusion hung over their heads because that past Tuesday a car had gone through a stop sign, T-boned the car of a family in this body, and killed the pregnant wife and her baby.

The chairs were set up in circles and people took their seats. The uneasy silence was broken by a simple prayer asking for Jesus' help. Despite the emotional chemistry going on among everyone in the room, it was in such a gathering as this that the Lord Jesus flowed freely through the saints! It was absolutely amazing. The singing was charged. The believers began to express Christ from their hearts with love and tears.

Then the bereaved husband stood up from his seat and opened his heart to those around him. Given the fresh wounds that had just come upon him, his words were incredibly appropriate, penetrating and moving. He spoke of Job's losses and his own in a beautiful way that exalted Jesus Christ. Such candor on his part could only happen in a community where deepening relationships existed.

The family we came with had to leave before the meeting was fully over. When we got into the Volkswagen bus and the engine started, I realized I was numb, but in the best sense. Words would be hard to find to express what had just happened when those saints came together. We had just experienced an unbelievable manifestation of Christ through His body—yet everything on the human level had gone very much awry.

Using this story as a spring board, I want to share a few of many perspectives that are vital in considering how we express Christ together.

1. *Be careful not to put much stock in the physical elements that surround our getting together in Christ.* It's not about planning, picking the right song, or anything else on the human level. I am not saying that all planning is wrong. The issue must be that we wish for Christ to lead by His Spirit. It is just too easy to rely on doing things in a certain way—the way we did things last week, and the week before. The Spirit is wind, not concrete.

2. *While not a pleasant thought, we must embrace the reality that community life is enhanced as Christ is glorified through our trials.* In the tragedy that occurred in the group we visited, Jesus was vibrantly expressed through the husband, and through the community as they came alongside him. One of the marks of ekklesia-life in this age is to participate in the sufferings of Christ. Suffering precedes glory.

3. *Christ's expression comes to settings where people pursue Him, not human agendas* (whether overt or covert). What a blessing to have people come together who are willing to shelve their preferences and opinions, and be satisfied with Jesus Christ alone. Nothing kills the flow of the Lord like individuals wearing their convictions and agendas on their sleeve.

4. *Christ manifests Himself among humble people.* "God resists the proud." Nothing grieves the Spirit more than pride. There is no telling what the Lord can do

in a group of people who are "low to the ground," not in the sense of groveling, but in the sense that they know well their need of Jesus and His followers. As Thomas Dubay put it beautifully, "In order to listen to others we need to be humble, small in our own estimation. Finding the solution to a math problem is possible without humility, but finding God's will is impossible without this virtue."

5. *Christ is expressed most pointedly when we enter into the burdens of others.* In the story above, this group was faced with coming alongside the husband for an extended period of caring. Paul said in Galatians 6:2, "Bear one another's burdens, and so fulfill the law of Christ." If our New Testament was burned up, and only this verse was left, we would have more than enough for Christ to work through us for the rest of our days. Paul also said, "Do good to everyone, especially the household of faith" (Gal. 6:10). When the Son of Man comes in glory, He will say to those who fed, clothed and visited others, "You did it to Me."

Because Christ is in each believer, the assumption is that they, as Paul put it, have a manifestation of the Spirit for benefit of the *ekklesia.* The most oft-repeated promise in the New Testament is that the Spirit in Christ's people will result in rivers of living water springing up within them. The Son having returned to the Father, it is now God's will for Christ to be expressed on earth through the *ekklesia.*

We know painfully well that there are obstacles and challenges to Christ being expressed through people like us. We can all be like porcupines. What, therefore, is our hope? Well, as I have often said, we must find hope in the sure promise of Jesus:

Which of you fathers, if your son asks for a fish, will give him a snake instead? Or if he asks for an egg, will give him a scorpion? If you then, though you are evil, know how to give good gifts to your children, how much more will your Father in heaven give the Holy Spirit to those who ask Him? (Luke 11:11-12)

As Christ's body on earth, we must never forget that our key posture is that of a branch abiding in the Vine. If His living water is impeded, it is not a new or better method or formula we need, or a prophecy conference, but rather to ask ourselves, "Are we abiding in Jesus our Vine?" We must not forget that without Him we can do nothing. Fruitfulness only results from us resting in Him.

Chapter 9

Poured Out

Jesus loves a free atmosphere where He can flow through His people with no hindrances. Amazing revelations of Him happen in an open, Spirit-led gathering. This happened to us recently on a Sunday morning when we were eating together and remembering the Lord.

Our sweet time together shifted gears suddenly. We each had sipped some wine from the pewter goblet. Dale picked it up, poured some wine out onto the table, and said with conviction,

"His crucifixion was not neat, it was very messy." We were all stunned for a few moments as we gazed at the liquid on the table and reflected on the words he had spoken. Then I said, "Crucifixion is chaotic, unpredictable and violent." We began to reflect on the great amounts of blood spilled in the sacrificial system of the Israelites. Nancy Leigh DeMoss has captured some key thoughts about the lambs led to the slaughter:

> It's been calculated that over the course of one year, 1,086 lambs were sacrificed in these regular recurring rhythm of offerings. And that's in addition to other offerings that were made for individual and corporate sin. That's a lot of lambs being slain. That's a lot of blood being shed. Lambs killed. Innocent, young, male lambs without blemish slain, killed, slaughtered, and their blood running through the tabernacle. The historian, Josephus, tells us that in the time of Christ during the Passover that there would be a quarter of a million Passover lambs that were slaughtered. And the blood of those lambs would flow out through viaducts down into the river, the brook Kidron. As those lambs were being slaughtered on that Passover, a carpenter from Nazareth named Jesus was put to death on a hill outside Jerusalem as the blood of God's Passover Lamb ran down from His hands and head and feet onto the ground below. ("Lamb of God," April 17, 2014, https://www.reviveourhearts.com/podcast/revive-our-hearts/lamb-god-1)

I think we often picture Jesus' crucifixion as an orderly event that went through various steps until He was left hanging on a tree with two others. There is, however, no polite way to pound crude stakes into human wrists and ankles. There would be blood everywhere in the vicinity of the tree. The jarring nature of the crucifixion does not mesh well with the "comfortable Christianity" most are used to. When Dale poured that wine out onto the table the Spirit of God deeply gripped us with the unbelievable ugliness of that day on Golgotha. He was *in our place* as our *substitute* and when He died, we died with Him. Jesus was *poured out* as a love offering on our behalf.

I took a picture of the wine on the table. It was not until 1968 that archaeological evidence was found that showed an aspect of the horror of crucifixion, and it is pictured below.

On the Mount of Olives He purchased the *ekklesia* of God with His own blood. We do not, therefore, belong to ourselves, but to Him who gave Himself for us. Given what He endured in crucifixion, it is no wonder that He asked Father if He could avoid this cup of suffering. It was not a pretty day. It was for sure a violent day. But because the kernel of wheat fell into the ground and died, Christ has blossomed all over the world.

In most settings of "the Lord's Supper," what Dale did would be condemned as sacrilegious. In an atmosphere where Jesus was welcome it became a powerful illustration of the supreme act of love accomplished in the midst of raw hostility.

Figure 14. Remains of the crucified Yehochanan: the ankle bone with stake still in place.

"But there are no explicit descriptions of how crucifixion was done. Until fairly recently there was not a single piece of archaeological evidence to explain the practice. In 1968, however, a significant archaeological discovery was made in a suburb of Jerusalem: an ossuary with the skeletal remains of a man named Yehochanan who had been crucified. Yehochanan had been nailed to an upright beam of wood through the ankle, but the nail hit a knot in the wood and bent, making it difficult to be removed after his death. And so a chunk of the wood was broken off, and Yehochanan was buried with wood and nail still attached to the ankle bone." – Bart Ehrman, *The New Testament: A Historical Introduction to the Early Christian Writings*, 3rd Edition, Oxford, 2004, p. 156.

Chapter 10

Community in the Raw

It will be illuminating to look briefly at a Christian community that began southeast of Americus in southern Georgia. Clarence Jordan and his wife, Florence, along with another Baptist family, the Englands, began Koinonia Farm in 1942. Their goal was to proclaim Jesus Christ and His teachings in a setting where people of any race could be taught productive farming and where community life could emerge around Jesus.

As a high school graduate, and having seen the gross mistreatment of Blacks (by White men who sang "Love Lifted Me" in church), Clarence knew that he wanted to be a scientific farmer who would help the poor have a better life. He went off to the state agricultural college in Athens.

From 1933-1939, he studied at the Southern Baptist Seminary in Louisville, Kentucky, where he obtained a Ph.D. in Greek New Testament. This was a strange background for an agrarian radical, but he knew what he would face ministering in the South. He would go on to publish many smaller volumes of *The Cotton Patch Version* of the New Testament (*CPV*), which placed the First Century setting into Southern America (e.g., Jesus was wrapped in a blanket and placed in an apple crate at his birth, lynched in Leesburg, Georgia and greets his disciples with a "Howdy" when he emerges from his tomb on Easter.)

So, in 1942, as America was preparing for a world war, Koinonia Farm began on a site of 440 acres. From the beginning, in their functioning together no one would view their possessions as their own, and race would not be a consideration of who would be part of the venture. Clarence translated Ephesians 3:6 as "The secret [mystery] is that the Negroes are fellow partners and equal members, co-sharers in the privileges of the gospel of Jesus Christ" (*CPV*). Needless to say, this did not sit well with Whites in Georgia.

The community waxed and waned. Some people came for a while, and others stayed. The fierce opposition did not appear until years later. Not surprisingly, resistance first came from religious people. In 1950 Rehoboth Baptist excommunicated its Koinonia Farm members because "said members have persisted in holding services where both white and colored attend together." After this happened the Jordans never tried to join another church. When asked his denomination, Clarence would happily reply, "Exbaptist."

The opposition from the broader White community in Sumter County became very violent, making national news. Koinonia Farm was accused of being Communist inspired. The Farm received threatening phone calls, experienced bombings, vandalism, Klan caravans, and some members were beaten. There were rifle, pistol and buckshot shootings at Koinonia houses, farm animals and residents. Insurance companies canceled all Farm policies. Koinonians could not sell their peanuts or buy gasoline for their tractors. No bank would handle their account, and no butane dealer would deliver fuel. The Farm community residents responded only by speaking peaceably to their assailants. They lived in nightly fear, however.

The Farm considered a move to a second headquarters in New Jersey, but it had to close. Christian community was as unwelcome in the North as it was in the South.

As we reflect on the events surrounding the Farm, we must return our thoughts again to Frank Viola's piece on the Cross. There is a cost to being a believing community, and it involves Christ's cross. An interchange Clarence had with his brother, Robert Jordan, in the early 1950's highlights the cost, which few are willing to pay. Clarence asked Robert to represent Koinonia legally.

"Clarence, I can't do that. You know my political aspirations. Why, if I represented you, I might lose my job, my house, everything I've got."

"We might lose everything too, Bob."

"It's different for you."

"Why is it different? I remember, it seems to me, that you and I joined the church the same Sunday, as boys. I expect when we came forward the preacher asked me about the same question he asked you. He asked me, 'Do you accept Jesus as your Lord and Savior?' And I said, 'Yes.' What did you say?"

"I follow Jesus, Clarence, up to a point."

"Could that point by any chance be—the cross?"

"That's right. I follow him to the cross, but not *on* the cross. I'm not getting myself crucified."

"Then I don't believe you are a disciple. You are an admirer of Jesus, but not a disciple of his. I think you ought to go back to the church you belong to, and tell them you're an admirer not a disciple."

"Well, now, if everyone who felt like I do did that, we wouldn't *have* a church, would we?"

"The question is," Clarence said, "Do you have a church?"

Clarence always connected following Jesus to the outworking of Christian community with others. But at the center of "fellowship" is the cost of Christ's cross. The tragic problem is that too many, like Robert Jordan, only want to follow Him "up to a point."

Clarence died suddenly of heart failure in his translator's shack on the Farm, October 29, 1969, at age 57.

The information above is based on Chapter 5, "The Theory Tested: Clarence Leonard Jordan—Radical in Community," in *Biography as Theology*, James W. McClendon Jr., Abingdon, 2000, pp. 112-139.

Chapter 11

The Mind of Christ in Our Life Together: All of Christ Through All the Voices

The way church is usually practiced renders the "laity" passive. Those sitting in the pews are used to a select sub-group—the pastor, an elder board, a deacon board—making key decisions for the church and then telling the membership what was decided.

But what happens when believers gather in settings where traditional leadership categories are absent? How are decisions made in groups where everyone participates in body-life?

In order to respond to these questions we must take a closer look at the word Jesus used in connection with His purpose—"I will build my *ekklesia*." "Called out ones" is the basic meaning of *ekklesia*, but that thought only scratches the surface of the word's significance.

In the Greek world *ekklesia* had a political dimension—"a duly called assembly." When the Old Testament was translated into Greek at the request of a secular ruler (in what came to be called the *Septuagint*), *ekklesia* was used to translate the Hebrew word *qahal*, referring to Israel as a gathered assembly.

"Church" is a horrible, misleading translation of *ekklesia* (cf., *Jesus Is* Family, Chapter 5, "Family Is *Ekklesia*," pp. 31-35). Every time the saints gather they are meeting to pursue the King— they meet around the King, the King is in their midst, and the King is in each believer.

In light of these perspectives, we need to get away from the idea—a notion certainly embedded in the institutional church—that we have two kinds of meetings: "worship services" and "business meetings." No. Our shared life together in Christ is rooted in our *one-ness* with Him and all the saints. This *one-ness* ("consensus," if you will) is expressed together whether we are singing or involved in decision-making. *One-ness* should permeate our very existence in Him.

The remainder of this chapter, then, will focus on our oneness as it pertains to the importance of *all voices being heard in the pursuit of Christ's will.*

As I have traveled among all kinds of fellowships since 1977, the number one concern that has come from the saints' hearts has been expressed in statements like—"a few voices have the clout, the rest don't matter," "no one has ever asked for my thoughts," "I felt ignored or put down when I questioned things," "sometimes the body would move so fast that I felt left in the dust," "I was told to go with the flow and not differ," and "when I asked myself, 'How could my concerns be processed in this body?' my mind was blank." Such sentiments indicate that things are going on that are diametrically opposed to Christ's heart.

The way of Jesus is radically "other" than what most of us have experienced. To Christ, every person and their voice is precious and significant. In His body, no one should fall through the cracks or feel like they are worthless. The easy way is to let one or a few give direction. The way of the Cross is for the body to hear Him by caring about what every person has to bring of Christ. As Thomas Dubay said, "A caring community is a listening community.".

As body-life is incarnated, one of the most important matters a group must process is *how to work things out together.* In 1 Corinthians 1 Paul confronts the assembly about their divisions and tells them to be "joined together" in the same mind concerning this problem. The verb "joined together" means to repair something that is torn, like mending a fishing net.

We don't know the details, but in order for this to happen, the Corinthians would have to all come together (after already having divided by clustering around various personalities) and hear the voice of Christ as it came through Paul. Given what we know about humans, coming to "one mind" would not occur by the wave of a wand, but by honest mutual discussion with a view toward following Jesus and forsaking divisions.

In dealing with the Corinthian problems, Paul does not address "leaders," but the whole body. The point being that in addressing any concern in the body, *coming to peace in His will must involve listening to and processing what Christ expresses through every brother and sister.* (Note: this does not mean that every person must say something; it does mean that there is a loving atmosphere in which any one can express themselves and expect their input to be listened to and processed).

Obviously, in traditional churches this is a monumental problem. Only certain voices are treated as important, and most voices are muted. The "will of God" is announced to a group by leaders. The great bulk of the members are not involved in the decision-making process. Their perspectives are never requested or taken seriously.

In Christ's *ekklesias* this model must be rejected and avoided. To Jesus, each of His sheep are a conduit through which He speaks. They must all be heard. To cite Thomas Dubay again, he amplifies this truth:

> The person speaking is important, even precious. We pay atten-
> tion to important people. To the proud person others are not
> important and so he is not inclined to take them that seriously.
> Even more, we value the opinions of those we love. If I do not
> really care what my brother/sister thinks, I had better doubt
> that I love them.

Every voice must be prized and sought after because Christ's mind will not reside in the same few, but among the many. As Dubay points out, "in community no one may assume that he/she alone can speak for God. No one can claim a wholeness of insight into the community's problems. This is why all must contribute their gifts, their charisms, their experience in shared dialog."

Let me share an event that happened in a hospital in 1982 to illustrate the importance of every voice being considered. A person in our fellowship had a serious heart issue, and the family and Dotty and I were in a room waiting for the doctor to speak with us before he was released. The doctor came in and gave some final words, which included that he should avoid the caffeine in dark sodas like Pepsi and Coke. I piped up and said that some light-colored sodas like Mountain Dew contained caffeine too. At first the doctor resisted my suggestion, but said he would look into it. The point being that the doctor could run circles around me concerning knowledge of the human body, but I had an important piece of information for this patient that was unknown to him. Vital perspective can come the most unexpected sources! "Out of the mouth of babies ... "

In light of these few, pointed thoughts, would it not be healthy for a group to come into the presence of Jesus and one another and candidly respond to such questions as these?

- Do we have an open, welcoming atmosphere in which all feel safe in sharing their portion of Christ?

- Have there been occasions when some contributions have been silenced by being put down or intimidated? As Frank Viola pointed out, when we gaze into the eyes of another believer, we are looking at Christ. Remember, then, if we demean or are rude to a brother or sister, we are speaking/acting directly to our Lord.

- Do all feel that their voices have been encouraged, solicited, listened to and processed in the decision-making process?

- Does the group feel like they are not moving together on anything until His peace descends on them with one-mindedness, or is there a sense that at times things are pressured and rushed through?

- Is care taken to make sure that communication of body issues has reached everyone, and that time has been given for questions, exploration and clarification to take place?

- Do the brothers and sisters feel that Christ's leadership is being expressed freely through everyone, or is it defaulting over time to some in the body?

- Does each believer display through Christ in them that they are eager to hear and respond to the concerns, the perspectives, the voice and the heart of every brother and sister?

- How can we expect to discover the Lord's mind in our midst if we do not honor, defer to, and submit to our Christ in each other?

- When the sun goes down, if all voices are not solicited, heard and processed the will of Christ will remain unknown to that group. Anything that hinders the free expression of all voices must be challenged.

Expanded thoughts from the "Consensus" Break-Out at Interconnect, July, 2013, Nashville; see also, Howard H. Brinton, *Reaching Decisions: The Quaker Method*, Pendle Hill Pamphlet, #65, February, 1952, 30pp.

Chapter 12

What Stands in the Way of Christ's Expression in His Body More Than This?

Chapter 5 of *Pagan Christianity* (Barna/Viola) is titled "The Pastor: Obstacle to Every-Member Functioning." No matter what angle you explore, traditional Christianity boils down to an unhealthy dependence on "the pastor," and on his or her gifts and vision. *Ministry* magazine asserted in 2010, "The local church pastor is key—absolutely central—to everything we are and do as a church." Julia McMillan in her book *Prophetic Crack* expressed the conviction of most church-goers: "*There is one primary voice in leadership. Where there is a pastor, that should be the only decisive voice that we hear. He is charged with soul care and is the ultimate voice the congregants expect to hear, especially regarding matters of vision and direction for the church*" (p. 105).

John Piper wrote a book called *Brothers, We Are Not Professionals*. The huge problem, however, is that pastors are in a system that encourages, and for the most part includes professionalism. Look at the multitude of advertisements in Christian magazines that promote the pastor's "career" and need for more academic degrees to enhance his/her ministry.

One could rightfully ask, "Where in the New Testament would this pastor centrality/dependence be found?" Julia encourages us to be informed by "the Word of God" (p. 112), but her sentiments about the pastor being "the one decisive voice we hear" falls into the category of errant human traditions that nullify the purposes of the Lord. The next chapter will show how we have built an infrastructure of "church" on a ghost that is nowhere to be found in the New Testament.

We will never have Christ-centered community where the 58 one anothers found in the New Testament can freely come to expression until the traditional pastor centrality is jettisoned.

Chapter 13

When Are We Going to Wake Up to Reality? The Nightmare of the Pastoral Institution

Mark Galli, Editor of *Christianity Today* has given us another article in a string of many that candidly lays out some serious problems resident in the traditional one-pastor system It is titled,

"The Most Risky Profession: Why you need to pray desperately for your pastor."

Notice the near-fatal weaknesses Mark points out in the American pastoral institution:

- "The state of the modern American pastorate has been shaped so that these sins—especially pride and hypocrisy—are impossible to escape."

- "[Pastors] are in a profession that is about as morally risky as they come."

- "American churches exalt and isolate their leaders almost by design."

- "Churches … like to know that someone is in charge, that someone is attending to the details, that someone is getting things done. That's why they've hired this dynamic, forward looking, administratively savvy leader."

- "[There] is the expectation that he also be the cathartic head of the church … someone to whom they can relate—at a distance. This is key, because the pastor has time to relate to very, very few members."

- "Most pastors have become heads of personality cults. Churches become identified more with the pastor—this is Such-and-Such's church—than anything larger. When the pastor leaves, or is forced to leave, it's devastating. It feels like a divorce . . ."

- "No wonder pastors complain about how lonely and isolated they feel."

- "He's stuck in a religious system from which few escape unscathed."

(Mark Galli, "The Most Risky Profession: Why You Need to Pray Desperately for Your Pastor," *Christianity Today*, August 8, 2011, http://www.christianitytoday.com/ct/2011/julyweb-only/mostriskyprofession.html?start=1).

When I read surveys of the pastoral landscape like Mark has given us, I feel burdened because there is something huge that is glaringly absent from the books and articles about "the pastor," multi-pastors and plurality of pastors. *They all assume that the one-pastor system we function under is what we must work with, and we just need to put band aids on it to make it all better.*

This is a fatal assumption that we must jettison. Mark notes that "shepherd" is "the biblical word for this position." But the truth is, the traditional notion of "the pastor" cannot be found in the narrative unfolded in the New Testament. *There is nothing in the New Testament about the "position" of pastor created by church traditions.*

Since this is true, then here are the questions we should really be dealing with:

- Why do we nullify the Word of God by our traditions? The pastoral position originates in the minds of people, not the Lord.

- *Why do we put unbearable burdens and expectations on "the pastor," when this is an "office" unknown in the New Testament?*

- *When will we stop hurting those in the "clergy" by continuing a system that is out of touch with Christ's revelation?*

- *When will we discontinue trying to fix or prop up a pastoral system that finds no merit in the New Testament?*

- If a patient had gum cancer and a doctor advised him that the solution was to brush his teeth thirty-two times a day, we would call that insanity. *Why, then, do we do the same thing by never examining the root problem of the one-pastor system, and assuming we just need a better spiritual toothbrush to get the nagging problems cleaned up?*

The root issue is that our practice of putting all our churchy eggs in the pastoral basket—essentially trying to build church upon the presence and expression of one gift—is a mistake of mammoth proportions, and is without biblical warrant. We need to be "radical," that is, *go to the root,* and cease the meaningless surface discussions that reinforce a hurtful system.

We need to eliminate the connection of service in the body of Christ with a "profession." Something is very wrong when being a pastor is a career choice. We need to pray desperately that the giftedness of the whole *ekklesia* will blossom in communities where the life of Christ is flowing like living waters.

Chapter 14

"Dear Pastor"? No, "Dear Saints"

With the inordinate emphasis that falls upon "the pastor" in churches, books, webinars, conferences, and DVDs, one might assume that the letters to the *ekklesias* began with, "Dear pastor, I have some matters to talk to you about … " *But they didn't.* The New Testament epistles are addressed *to the saints.* Even in a letter to an individual, Philemon, "beloved Apphia, Archippus and the *ekklesia* in your home" are mentioned.

The implications of this fact are staggering. Our practice is overwhelmingly weighted to *leaders,* but Paul addressed what the Lord gave him *to the body.* He believed a body of believers had the Spirit and Word of God, and so armed were capable of working through whatever they faced together. Paul reminds the Corinthians,

> "If any of you has a dispute with another, dare it be taken before the ungodly for judgment instead of before the saints? Do you not know that the saints will judge the world? And if you are to judge the world, are you not competent to judge trivial cases? Do you not know that we will judge angels? How much more the things of this life? Therefore, if you have disputes about such

matters, appoint as judges even people of little account in the *ekklesia.*"

Paul viewed the body of Christ as a Spirit-led setting in which to consider and resolve a wide range of issues that would come up in the course of their life together. The truth is, as you turn the pages in the New Testament there is very little said about elders, deacons, apostles, prophets, evangelists and teachers. Yes, they are mentioned occasionally, but the unmistakable revelation of the Lord concerns the 58 one anothers that dominate the NT landscape.

In Matthew 18:15-20, if a problem is not taken care of on a private or plural level, it is to be "told to the *ekklesia.*" Jesus saw the *body* as the final resting place for resolution. Most people think, "If there is problem, take it to the leaders for them to deal with." But Jesus saw the body handling issues with His light as part of a "binding and loosing" process—to allow or deny various activities. Interestingly, in the Jewish culture, "binding and loosing" was a practice limited to the religious leaders, the Rabbis, Scribes and Pharisees. For example, a troubled Jew might ask a Rabbi, "How far can I travel on the Sabbath?" The Rabbi's answer would be an instance of "binding and loosing." But in Jesus' kingdom *all of His followers participate* in "binding and loosing," as He revealed in Matthew 18.

Paul's *body-saturated* view of life in Christ is a game-changer. Life in Christ is not "me-and-Jesus," but "Jesus-in-me-and-my-brothers and sisters" (1 Cor. 12:13). When you think about it, the NT imperatives ("be kind to one another," "forgive as Christ forgave you," etc.) are meaningless without the assumption of *local committed relationships.* You can't be long-suffering with a rock, but you can be with a person you know. Paul could write letters to specific bodies of saints in cities and locales. They were focused on Christ and carrying out His affairs together.

Paul knew nothing about "the pastor," but he did have confidence in the saints—the ones who would judge the world and angels!

Chapter 15

"One Anothers" Everywhere!

Drawing by Megan Cronje

Even though there are 58 one anothers in the New Testament, our church practice makes it look like the body is one part, not many. In most churches you simply do not see one-anothering dominating the landscape of church practice. No wonder, for most church structures do not encourage, foster, cultivate and make provision for deepening relationships.

If these relational one-anothers are not flowing with Christ's life in the body, is it any surprise that so much division, confusion and disruption reigns in churches?

Why do the one-anothers permeate the New Testament? The answer is simple. The Lord came to earth to fulfill the Father's eternal purpose to create a *new Adam*, a new race, where there is no male, female, Jew, Greek, bond or free, Barbarian or Scythian. This is Christ's body on earth. These very diverse groups were made one in Jesus *by His cross*. As His crucifixion drew near, He proclaimed, "A new command I give you, Love *one another*. As I have loved you [on the cross], so you must love *one another*. By this everyone will know you are My disciples, if you love *one another.*" Thus, all the other one-anothers flow out of His singular command to love each other as He loved us on Golgotha.

Jesus knew that His cross would result in face-to-face communities in places all over the First Century world. He knew that diverse believers coming together in fellowship would be dicey and messy. Thus, the one anothers appeared in the New Covenant writings as exhortations about how to live with others in light of Jesus' life in them. These one anothers would indicate that vital body-life was taking place beyond just their gatherings as a group—"exhort one another daily" (Heb. 3:13).

Let's look specifically at some of the one anothers found in the New Testament for our encouragement. Many believers have not even thought about how the one anothers are on the right hand and the left.

- "Have salt in yourselves, and be at peace with one another" (Mark 9:50). Like any of us in the Body of Christ, the disciples could get on each other's nerves. But Jesus said, "blessed are the peacemakers."

- "So we, being many, are one body in Christ, and each one parts of one another … in honor preferring one another … be of the same mind toward one another" (Romans 12:5, 10, 16). These words underscore the intimate relationship believers have with each other. As Frank Viola astutely pointed out: "When we deal with a brother and sister in Christ, we are not merely dealing with another human being. We are dealing with the parts of Jesus Christ. We are handling Christ. We are handling the members of Christ. For they have been made a part of Him. Put differently, when we look into the eyes of a fellow Christian, we meet the gaze of Jesus Christ Himself."

- "Let us not therefore judge one another any more" (Romans 14:13). In this context, Paul is dealing with how differences over meats, drinks and observing days can cause strife in the body. He simply tells them that in matters of liberty and conscience they must stop passing judgment on those who differ from their convictions.

- There is an important nuance that must be noted. If anyone takes something that is "nothing," like circumcision, and makes it mandatory, they have crossed a line that must be confronted.

- "Wherefore receive one another, as Christ also received us to the glory of God" (Romans 15:7). Because they have been accepted by God without qualifications, they must extend acceptance also to the brothers and sisters, even if they differ in non-critical areas.

- "You, my brothers and sisters, are also able to admonish one another" (Romans 15:14). Because there are relationships present, the brethren can speak into each other's lives in appropriate ways. To accept one another without the possibility of dealing with concerns is mushy sentimentality; to try and correct others without acceptance will turn into a witch-hunt.

- "You have been called to liberty; do not use your liberty as an occasion to the flesh, but by love serve one another … Bear one another's burdens and thus fulfill the law of Christ" (Galatians 5:13, 6:2). The false teachers were asking the Galatians to bear the brunt of the law, which no one can bear/fulfill and results in curse. Paul asks them to bear the burdens of others and thus fully fulfill the law of Christ, which is "love one another as I have loved you."

- "Forgiving one another, even as God for Christ's sake forgave you" (Ephesians 4:32). The benchmark of everything is Christ. How can we choke someone who owes us a dollar, when Jesus has forgiven us millions of dollars?

- "Being subject to one another in the fear of Christ" (Ephesians 5:21). The body of Christ has no place for one or some to be "over" and above the others. We are to submit (that is, defer, listen) to one another with reference to Jesus as our Leader. Adam was not put "over" Eve. Together, they were both given dominion over the earth, not over other people.

- "See to it that none of you has a sinful, unbelieving heart that turns away from the living God. But encourage one another daily, as long as it is called Today, so that none of you may be hardened by sin's deceitfulness" (Hebrews 3:12-13). The antidote to apostasy and being tricked by sin is *a lifestyle of mutual encouragement with others*. Do you see this as vital in your life? "Daily" certainly implies rubbing shoulders with others in relationships outside meetings of the whole group. Ideally, this should occur spontaneously as we see the need for ongoing body-life together.

- "And let us consider how we may spur one another on to love and good deeds" (Hebrews 10:24). The word "consider" means to give deliberate, intentional mental attention to something, in this case other brothers and sisters. How much time do we devote to thinking of how we might encourage the brethren in the things of Christ?

- "Let us not cease meeting together, as some are in the habit of doing, but let us encourage one another—and all the more as you see the Day approaching" (Hebrews 10:25). In this verse, the mutual encouragement is given in the gatherings of the body. This implies that the meetings were open to the Lord's leading and to the participation of all present. However, we must be careful not to be meeting-centric. The gathering of the body, "when you come together as an *ekklesia*," will only be deepened and enhanced if there are daily face-to-face encounters that occur in the outworking of body-life.

Paul indicated that in a gathering of the saints where all can "prophesy one by one," some powerful effects can result in people's lives. "So if the whole *ekklesia* comes together and everyone speaks in tongues, and some who do not understand or some unbelievers come in, will they not say that you are out of your mind? But if an unbeliever or someone who does not understand comes in while everyone is prophesying, they will be convinced by all that they are sinners and will be judged by all, and the secrets of their heart will be laid bare. So they will fall down and worship God, exclaiming, 'God is really among you'" (1 Cor. 14:23-25).

There is no formula for Christ expressing Himself through His people. It can occur in a million ways. The body is free to give Him creative expression through endless avenues.

We've all heard about endless conferences on prophecy and church leadership, but have you ever heard of a conference dealing with the 58 one anothers? Have you ever heard a series of sermons on the one anothers? This illustrates how far afield we are. We focus attention on that for which there is scanty evidence, and by so doing pass by that for which there is abundant revelation.

Again, if you listen carefully to today's Bible teaching, you'll probably find that most preachers are clueless regarding the one-anothers and how they undergird the New Testament writings.

Chapter 16

Saints are "Overseers"

Traditionally, "leaders" in the New Testament are called "elders" and "overseers." The King James Version (1611) translates "overseer" as "bishop." The Greek word for "overseer"/bishop is *episcopos* (from which we derive the word, "episcopal"). It must be underscored that historically in Bible translations this word is linked to *leadership*. What has been largely missed in translations is the form of *episcopos* that was used in Hebrews 12:15: "Look after each other [*episkopountes*] so that none of you fails to receive the grace of God. Watch out that no poisonous root of bitterness grows up to trouble you, corrupting many" (*New Living Translation*). In this verse, then, the *whole body* is included in the "oversight" of one another.

Lutheran scholar, R.C.H. Lenski, noted, "*Episcopos* is a bishop; the participle bids all the readers to act as part of the *episcopoi*, overseers, by exercising continuous oversight of each other" (*The Interpretation of Hebrews*, p. 443).

The *ekklesia* is to care so deeply for each other that they oversee (watch over) to make sure everyone is walking in God's grace. William Barclay noted, "the early Greek commentator, Theophylact, interprets this in terms of a journey of a band of travelers who every now and again check up, 'Has anyone fallen out? Has anyone been left behind while the others have pressed on?'" (*The Letter to the Hebrews*, Revised Edition, 1976, p. 182).

We are used to thinking that clergy paid for their services are "overseers." However, such an outlook cannot be sustained in light of the *body-oversight* unveiled in Hebrews 12:15.

Chapter 17

The Lord Sets the Lonely in Families

Being Christ on earth, we have the joyous privilege of continuing His compassionate service to the marginalized poor, needy and the sick. More than anything else, Jesus was marked as a "friend of 'sinners.'"

> Then it happened that as Jesus was reclining *at the table* in the house, behold, many tax collectors and sinners came and *began* dining with Jesus and His disciples [presumably at Matthew's home]. And when the Pharisees saw *this*, they said to His disciples, "Why is your Teacher eating with the tax collectors and sinners?" But when *Jesus* heard *this*, He said, "*It is* not those who are healthy who need a physician, but those who are sick. Now go and learn what this means: 'I desire compassion, rather than sacrifice,' for I did not come to call the righteous, but sinners." (Matthew 9:10-13)

> "The Son of Man has come eating and drinking, and you say, 'Behold, a gluttonous man and a drunkard, a friend of tax collectors and sinners!'" (Luke 7:34)

As Jesus walked among people in the First Century, the sick, the needy, the beggars and the broken were constantly in His eyesight. He responded with compassion and healing. Likewise, as Christ on earth now, His body is to continue Jesus' ministry of caring for others.

It appears that the far-reaching effects of the political and medical upheavals of 2020 are ill-affecting the public much more than we may realize. Many cultural pressures have served to separate people to the point where our generation has sunk into a terrible malaise—*loneliness*. Conan Milner noted in his article, "The Impact of Loneliness":

> DeLuca says "Loneliness … is a very overwhelming emotion because it goes against what we are as human beings" … People are, by nature, social creatures … Erin Cantor says that the root of loneliness is a feeling that you don't belong and that you lack true meaningful connection … Cantor says that people who fail to find meaningful connections for an extended period of time can give up in frustration, cutting themselves off even more … Cantor said, "There really is a double pandemic of loneliness and COVID-19, and the long-term mental health effects of our social distancing and isolation are going to be very, very damaging" … Wellness writer Melanie Musson says she felt the "sting of isolation" as she was going through the last couple of months of her pregnancy. It was during her state's imposed shut down. She said her body craved human connection. Thankfully, friends came to her rescue. "Shortly before my baby was born, two friends of mine knocked at the door. I hadn't had in-person interaction with anyone for over a month. I didn't even know how to handle a knock at the door. When I realized it was my friends and they had brought me treats, I asked if I could please hug them. I hadn't touched anyone outside my immediate family in weeks. I am not a hugger, but I needed human touch" … What we really need, and thrive on, are genuine in-person connections. And a lack of this vital human interaction may be affecting us more deeply than we imagine … When real people are not available, people often turn to animals. DeLuca says that caring for another living being, even if it is just a plant or fish, can make a big difference in our mental well-being (*The Epoch Times*, November 5-10, 2020, pp. 1, 6; cf. Bowen Xiao, "Mother

Loses Son to Overdose, Warns of Impact of Pandemic," *Epoch Times*, May 26-June 1, 2021, pp. A1, A6-7).

In times like these, shouldn't believers as individuals and families, and as believing communities *be there* for the many hurting people that surround us? How can we carry on the healing ministry of Christ on earth? At a minimum, shouldn't we reach out to the needy ones that the Lord brings into our pathway? Paul urged us, "as we have opportunity, let us do good to everyone, especially to those who belong to the family of believers."

The New Testament presents *hospitality* as a natural way for us to care for others and develop relationships. Henri Nouwen in his 1975 book, *Reaching Out*, saw hospitality as a lens through which to view all of our relationships—husband/wife, parents/children, teachers/students and healers/patients. Hospitality, he said is "primarily the creation of a free space where the stranger can enter and become a friend instead of an enemy. Hospitality is not to change people, but to offer them space where change can take place ... we can offer a space where people are encouraged to disarm themselves, to lay aside their occupations and preoccupations ... Just as we cannot force a plant to grow, but can take away the weeds and stones which prevent its development, so we cannot force anyone to such a personal and intimate change of heart, but we can offer the space where such a change can take place."

Nouwen suggested that we all desperately need the hospitality of free space in order to grow in Christ: "if we expect any salvation, redemption, healing and new life, *the first thing we need is an open receptive place where something can happen to us ...* "

Christ offers us open hospitality when we gather as His house. The atmosphere He engenders is accepting, non-condemning, non-judgmental, caring and compassionate. The issue is, *Are we passionate about participating in and contributing to such an open, receptive setting with other believers and neighbors where we live?*

Can you begin to see the importance of viewing our life together in Christ through the lens of hospitality? *He graciously extends hospitality of free space to us, and we in turn extend open hospitality to others.* It is in this climate that we can be honest, be vulnerable and discover true growth as persons.

Thinking about hospitality leads us naturally to consider *safe places*. As image-bearers, each person has the innate desire to *be with* others. From another angle this translates into longing for a *safe place*.

What marked those healthy settings where we felt safe in our own life experiences? The key component was likely that we *felt accepted in those settings where we were loved without conditions.* Because of our fallen world, a lot of us were set back personally at different times in our lives because we sought to be, or were forced to be with others in very unsafe places—places where we were abused, exploited, wounded or manipulated. Is it any wonder that vast multitudes are gun-shy of relationships when their past tells them, as Henri Nouwen noted, "that there is no one who cares and offers love without conditions, and no place where we can be vulnerable without being used"? Whether they know it or not, *most people are looking for a safe place.* In fact, Henri Nouwen made the point that at the core of human existence is the need for a safe place. In this regard, each of us would do well to consider what Nouwen said in his talks on The Prodigal Son:

> What I'd like you to think about is that it is very, very important to feel safe. And one of the things that I'm more and more aware of is how important it is for you, for me, for us to have a safe place. Where can you be really safe? Somehow the spiritual

journey is a journey that requires that we have a deep, deep sense of safety.

And I do hope that you discover more and more where it's safe for you. We have to start discovering that safety with each other, in nature, you have to discover that safety in the physical space where you are, you have to discover that safety in prayer, and you have to discover that safety with God.

And my deepest conviction is that once you have a place where you are safe, that's the place where you always can return. But if you don't have a safe place to return to, all of your life becomes scary, because you never know where to go back to.

And all I want to do in this series on the Prodigal Son is to give you an image of safety, a return to the place where it is safe, and probably the most useful word for that is 'womb,' the womb of God. That's the safest place. A lot of us weren't even safe in the womb because our mothers were sometimes also afraid, and somehow there is no human being who hasn't experienced very early on the fears of those around him or her. We carry that in our lives.

The spiritual life is to discover that there is safety for us. And that God wants to offer us that safe place where we can dwell, and where we can return to, and then we can let our whole body and mind and heart sort of stay without fear. And I'm really convinced that in order to be strong, to take risks, to do new things, we have to be able to be totally safe somewhere else where we can return to (Henri Nouwen, "The Return of the Prodigal Son," 1998, Tape #2, "The Older Son" [cassette]).

In the troubling times unfolding in our culture, will we ask the Lord to make us safe people and safe communities? Where will fellow humans find safe havens for comfort and healing in days of confusion, and perhaps even social chaos that may come?

Remember the Antonine Plague in AD 165-180. As Rodney Stark recalled in *The Rise of Christianity*, while pagan leaders, the general population, including physicians and nurses, fled for their safety, many Christians risked their lives and stayed in the afflicted cities to help the needy.

As we have reflected on hospitality and safe places, it remains for us to uncover a few thoughts about a crucial blind spot in our thinking about "church." We have forgotten Paul's description of the composition of the early *ekklesia*: "Think of what you were when you were called. Not many of you were wise by human standards; not many were influential; not many were of noble birth" (1 Cor. 1:26). The early *ekklesia* was made up mostly of the lower crust of society. Henri Nouwen saw the significance of this sociological reality.

> The most honored parts of the body are not the head or hands, which lead and control. The most important parts are the least presentable parts. That's the mystery of the Church. As people called out of oppression to freedom, we must recognize that it is the weakest among us—the elderly, the small children, the handicapped, the mentally ill, the hungry and sick—who form the real center. Paul says, "It is the parts of the body which we consider least dignified that we surround with the greatest dignity" (1 Corinthians 12:23). The Church as the people of God can truly embody the living Christ among us only when the poor remain its most treasured part. Care for the poor, therefore, is much more than Christian love. It is the essence of being the body of Christ … The poor make the Church faithful to its vocation. When the Church is no longer a church for the poor, it loses its spiritual identity. It gets caught up in disagreements, jealousy, power games and pettiness … The poor are given to the Church so that the Church as the body of Christ can be and remain a place of mutual concern, love, and peace … Thus we are called as members of the Church to keep going to the margins of our society (*Bread for the Journey*, HarperOne, 2006, October 30, 31, November 1).

The Lord's desire is for the lonely, broken ones to find family. Will we open our hearts, our homes, and our resources to help those in His house, and those looking for a safe place of love, acceptance and authenticity?

At the beginning, I mentioned that a pervasive sub-set of the Lord's heart is His care for orphans, widows, the fatherless and the oppressed. This truth opens the window for understanding why "care for the poor, therefore, is much more than Christian love. It is the essence of being the body of Christ" on earth (Nouwen).

Chapter 18

"Each and Every One of You Has A Song"

Paul told the Corinthians, "each and every one of you has a psalm [song]" (1 Corinthians 14:26). Religious tradition has been pulpit/sermon centered, and as a result the participation of the whole body, as described by Paul in 1 Corinthians 14, has been lost. Likewise, singing in the early church came to expression through the brothers and sisters in the gathering as "each and every one of you has a psalm [song]." Remember, they had no hymnals. They had no collection of Jesus songs to choose from. The songs sprang up from those present.

As history moved on, the church became more like an institution and less like a family. Just as the pulpit took the place of body participation, music moved "up front" in the form of choirs. A form of congregational singing appeared in the Protestant Reformation, but it was formal and scripted.

In the 1800s and 1900s hymnals became more common, and each denomination had their own collection of songs.

Since the 1960s many churches still have choirs, but more and more "worship bands" have become an established feature in religious services. Music in churches has moved "up front" for sure.

The 1970s until now has seen Contemporary Christian Music (CCM) explode commercially. Certainly much beautiful music has come forth from very gifted people.

But I think we must return to a basic question: is it possible we have forfeited tremendous blessings and hindered the expression of Jesus by eliminating rank-and-file believers as a primary source for music and songs?

Like it or not, we connect musical articulation to those who have some prowess in musical skills, even specific training for voice and instruments. Remember, however, that Paul's words, "each of you has a song," were addressed to people who, for the most part, were musically illiterate. In fact, 94% of all persons in the First Century were illiterate. This highlights the reality that Christ in the saints brought forth all kinds of utterances, including songs, to build up the *ekklesia*—by the Spirit, without formal training.

Paul also told the Corinthians, "each of you has a teaching." This does not mean that every person has the gift of teaching, but it does mean all can share in the teaching that goes on in an open meeting. Hebrews 5 said to the body, "when you should be teachers, you have need to be taught . . ." Recall that in Paul's thought even singing is "teaching" (Col. 3:16). So when he said that each one had a song, this does not mean all are gifted musically, but it does mean that as the Lord leads all can contribute to the musical expression in the body.

1 Corinthians 14:26 underscores the fact that traditional "worship services" are far afield from the openness Paul desired when he said, "you may all prophesy one by one." As R.C. Sproul confessed years ago, "in Protestant worship, for the most part, we sit and listen to a sermon." Paul envisioned a setting

much more robust than that—a body gathering where each one could bring their portion of Christ to the body-feast, eating and drinking of Christ.

Ask the Lord if there is not a song (or more) in you that Christ has purposed to be part of the grass that will help pasture His flock. Perhaps one has the words and another the melody. There are untold ways His songs can come to fruition. Frank Viola encouraged the saints at a 2007 Dallas, TX, conference:

> Let's raise the bar on the songs we sing in our house churches. The greatest songs I have ever sung in my life did not come from the Vineyard, they didn't come from Maranatha Music, or Integrity, or whoever you want to name. They came from the pen of brothers and sisters who were living in organic church life … who were non-professional musicians. They wrote them out of the soil of body life. And those songs (I am as honest as I can be) trump anything I've ever heard in the institutional church. Do you know that the early Christians wrote their own songs? Do you know they were profoundly Christ-centered? They had great depth, and they were experiential. They were written out of the soil of their experience of Christ in the body of Christ. Would to God that we would take our cue from the early Christians and write our own songs. Some of the songs that ordinary non-professional Christians have written will blow your mind. Home-grown songs, right out of the soil of the life of the church. Centered on Christ and with depth. It can be done. Brothers and sisters, I challenge you: Let's raise the bar. There are songs that are waiting to be written out of your experience of Christ in the church.

Why is "each one of you has a song" essentially meaningless now in groups of believers? Paul meant a whole lot more by that phrase than for a person to choose a song from a printed hymnal of some sort. Are we not missing a deep well of edification by relegating musical input to experts? Doesn't Paul's phrase imply a rich grassroots source for spiritual songs—the saints themselves?

Chapter 19

Do We Really Believe Who We Are?

Paul's approach to life in Christ boils down to this, "You are complete in Jesus, now live like it." "You have the Spirit, now walk in the Spirit." "He is in you, now walk in His life." "He is in the body, let each one then bring their portion of Jesus to the feast at the table."

As we have traveled through some of the Lord's word, we have seen some amazing, heart-stopping perspectives. His eternal purpose in the Son is unmistakable, and undergirds the course of history. It is hard to believe, but in this plan He views us as the apple of His eye. After Jesus ascended, He sees us as continuing Jesus' ministry on earth. He directs everything happening in the world with the *ekklesia* in view. He purposed for the *ekklesia* to be a counter-cultural display of His multi-faceted wisdom now, where the brothers and sisters bring their portion of the Lord—special, unique living water that only each one can bring to the table.

As the Psalmist declared, "such knowledge is too wonderful for me!" Do we really believe that through His eyes, He looks at His Bride in the outworking of His eternal purpose as *Christ on earth?* Are we asking Him to align our lives in line with His Son-driven heart?

If we are captured by Jesus as God's eternal purpose, we more than likely will have to turn our back on religious institutions, stifled by human traditions. Clyde Reid observed in 1966:

> The presence of God is not limited to the institutional structures, and to reject the institutional churches is not the same as rejecting God or rejecting the Christian faith. "Churchy" thinking is one of the great heresies of the modern church—the notion that unless one appears regularly in a certain kind of building labeled a Christian church, God has no relationship with them whatsoever. This is a manifestation of the current "preacher-cult" in which the clergy emphasize church attendance as the heart of the religious life, and thereby maintain a Sunday morning fan club. Some people may have to reject the churches to find Christ and vitality, for there are many churches where it is almost impossible to find or to recover that vitality. And God is surely present outside the churches—often more present without than within. God's Spirit is free in the world, and not captive in the churches. The Spirit of God has always resisted our efforts to put Him in a box and control our access to Him. The Spirit moves where He will, and sometimes he has to bypass the comfortable, respectable structures we call religious, and speak to us in fresh ways and unaccustomed tongues (*The God-Evaders*, Harper & Row, 1966).

Most people are accustomed only to religious models, so they cannot conceive of "doing church" without the inherited trappings—church building, pulpit, church bulletins, Sunday school, pews and hymnals. But once a revelation comes that we are Christ's body on earth, we can step out into a freedom in which we can "look after each other," and "each one of us can have a song, a word of instruction, a revelation, a tongue or an interpretation." We can be a *body*, instead of just one mouth speaking to many ears.

We have the sobering privilege of filling out the afflictions of Christ that are still lacking, for the sake of His body, which is the *ekklesia* (Col. 1:24). Christ continues His work on earth through us!

For Further Reflection

1. Howard H. Brinton, *Reaching Decisions: The Quaker Method*, Pendle Hill, #65, February, 1952, 30pp.

2. Emil Brunner, *The Misunderstanding of the Church*, Lutterworth Press, 1952, 132pp.

3. Watchman Nee, *Christ, The Sum of All Spiritual Things*, Christian Fellowship Publishers, 1973, 96pp.

4. Watchman Nee, *The Church in the Eternal Purpose of God*, CLC Publications, 1973, 238pp.

5. Henri Nouwen, *Reaching Out: The Three Movements of the Spiritual Life*, 1975.

6. Milt Rodriguez, *The Community Life of God*, The Rebuilders, 2009, 200pp.

7. T. Austin Sparks, "That They May All Be One," two volumes, 42 sessions, 1964, Philippines. https://www.austin-sparks.net/english/books/that_they_may_all_be_one_even_as_we_are_one_volume_1.html; https://www.austin-sparks.net/english/books/that_they_may_all_be_one_even_as_we_are_one_volume_2.html

8. Sherry Turkle, *Alone Together: Why We Expect More from Technology and Less from Each Other*, Basic Books, 2011, 360pp.

9. Frank Viola, *From Eternity to Here: Rediscovering the Ageless Purpose of God*, David C. Cook, 2009, 320pp.

10. John H. Yoder, *Body Politics: Five Practices of the Christian Community Before the Watching World*, Herald Press, 2001, 88pp.

11. Jon Zens, *Elusive Community: Why Do We Avoid What We Were Created For?* Quoir, 2020, 70pp.

12. Jon Zens, *Jesus Is Family: His Life Together*, Quoir, 2017, 104pp.

13. Jon Zens, *Life Between the Bookends—Is The Lord's Passion Our Passion Too?* Quoir, 2018, 35pp.

For more information about Jon Zens
or to contact him for speaking engagements,
please visit *www.SearchingTogether.org*

Many voices. One message.
Quoir is a boutique publishing company
with a single message: Christ is all.
Our books explore both His
cosmic nature and corporate expression.
For more information, please visit
www.quoir.com